INNOVATION THROUGH ADVERSITY

DID ANYTHING GOOD COME OUT OF

WORLD WAR I?

PHILIP STEELE

ROSEN
PUBLISHING®
New York

Published in 2016 by The Rosen Publishing Group, Inc.
29 East 21st Street, New York, NY 10010

Library of Congress Cataloging-in-Publication Data

Steele, Philip.
Did anything good come out of World War I?/Philip Steele.
pages cm.—(Innovation through adversity)
Includes bibliographical references and index.
ISBN 978-1-5081-7068-6 (library bound)
1. World War, 1914-1918—Influence—Juvenile literature.
2. World War, 1914-1918—Technology—Juvenile literature. I. Title.
D522.7.S744 2015
940.3'14—dc23
2015024635

Manufactured in the United States of America

The publisher would like to thank the following for their kind permission to reproduce their photographs:

Key: (t) top; (c) centre; (b) bottom; (l) left; (r) right

The following images are public domain:
4cl, 4–5c, 6bl, 8cl, 8b, 9tr, 9b, 10tl, 11c, 12tl, 12–13c, 13br, 14cl, 14–15c, 15tl tr, 18tl tr b, 19bl, 20tl, 20–21c, 21tc tr, 22tl, 22–23t, 23cr, 23bc, 24–25tc, 25tr bl br, 26t, 27tl tr br, 28cl tr, 29cr, 31cr br, 32c bl, 33tr, cr cl, 34br, 36bl cr, 37tl, 39tc br, 40bl, br, 43cr

All other images istock.com unless otherwise indicated.

Front Cover tl Shutterstock.com, bl Deutsches Uhrenmuseum
11tr German Federal Archive, 16b tr German Federal Archive, 19c German Federal Archive, 29c Corbis Images/Bettmann, 34bl Deutsches Uhrenmuseum, 34tr Shutterstock.com, 35 cr German Federal Archive, 37cr Getty Images/Popperfoto, 37bl Wellcome Trust, 38–39 bc Getty Images/Culture Club, 41 IWM/Getty Images, 43 t German Federal Archive.
Every attempt has been made to clear copyright. Should there be any inadvertent omission, please apply to the publisher for rectification.

The website addresses (URLs) included in this book were valid at the time of going to press. However, it is possible that contents or addresses may have changed since the publication of this book. No responsibility for any such changes can be accepted by either the author or the Publisher.

METRIC CONVERSION CHARTS

1 inch = 2.54 centimeters	1 mile = 1.609 kilometers
1 foot = 30.48 centimeters	1 cup = 250 milliliters
1 yard = .914 meters	1 ounce = 28 grams
1 square foot = .093 square meters	1 fluid ounce = 30 milliliters
1 square mile = 2.59 square kilometers	1 teaspoon = 5 milliliters
1 ton = .907 metric tons	1 tablespoon = 15 milliliters
1 pound = 454 grams	355 degrees F = 180 degrees Celsius

CONTENTS

DEATH IN NO–MAN'S LAND

All week, the big guns of the Allies had been pounding the German lines. After firing more than 1,700,000 shells, the artillery fell silent. Along the 21-mile (34-km) long front line of this offensive, British troops now stood in the mud-filled trenches with bayonets fixed to their rifles. They waited for the signal to attack. At last, they heard the shrill sound of the whistles and clambered out of the trenches to face the enemy guns. This was known as 'going over the top'.

WORLD WAR I FIGURES

NAME: **FIELD MARSHALL DOUGLAS HAIG**
LIVED: **1861–1928**
JOB: BRITISH COMMANDER ON THE WESTERN FRONT

In 1918, Haig led the British forces to a series of victories that helped defeat the Germans. However, the enormous casualties suffered at the Somme and later campaigns made him a highly controversial figure after the war.

THE FIRST BATTLE OF THE SOMME

GREAT
BRITAIN

GERMANY

Somme

FRANCE

The area between the Allied trenches and the German positions was called 'no-man's land'. This once peaceful farmland was now littered with broken trees and deep craters where shells had exploded. The advancing Allied soldiers immediately faced a hail of German machine gun fire. Many fell, wounded and dying. Some were caught on the barbed wire that guarded the German trenches – the Allied guns had failed to clear the way ahead of them. On that day alone about 20,000 British soldiers died and 40,000 more were wounded. It was July 1, 1916, halfway through World War I, which lasted from 1914–1918. The battle that started that day near the River Somme in France, raged until November 18. The Allies advanced just 7.5 miles (12 km). About 420,000 British, 200,000 French and some 500,000 Germans troops were wounded or killed.

"FOR A FULL WEEK WE WERE UNDER INCESSANT BOMBARDMENT. DAY AND NIGHT THE SHELLS CAME UPON US. OUR DUGOUTS CRUMBLED."

Trench warfare in 1916, as described by a German Medical Officer, Lt Stefan Westmann.

A British soldier keeps guard in a captured German trench during the Somme offensive.

HOW CAN ANYTHING GOOD COME OUT OF A WAR?

As World War I has become a lasting symbol of the horrors of warfare, it is worth asking what the aims of the conflict were and if they were achieved. Can we say whether any good at all came out of this terrible era? We shall see that some benefits did arise from the disaster, some lessons were learned and there were some useful innovations. But the terrible suffering and waste of life can hardly be seen as a justification for these advances,

COUNTDOWN TO CONFLICT

World War I, also known as the Great War, was the first truly global conflict. It involved countries and troops from six continents, although most of the fighting took place in western, southern and eastern Europe, in Egypt and in southwest Asia.

THE WORLD BEFORE THE WAR

During the 19th century, Europe went through many changes. Industrialization saw factories and big cities spread across the countryside. New nations, such as Italy and Germany in 1871, emerged as smaller territories joined together. These competed with long-established powers, such as France and Great Britain, for raw materials and overseas markets and to create worldwide empires. These nations became fierce rivals, leading to rising political tensions.

"THE LAMPS ARE GOING OUT ALL OVER EUROPE, WE SHALL NOT SEE THEM LIT AGAIN IN OUR LIFETIME."

Sir Edward Grey (right),
British Foreign Secretary,
August 1914.

1914

A CHAIN OF ALLIANCES

The European powers were involved in several alliances that would ultimately lead them to war. Germany was allied with Austria-Hungary and Italy (the Central powers), while Russia was allied with France and Great Britain (the Allied Powers). Germany was also in dispute with Russia over the small Balkan nations of southeast Europe. One of these, Bosnia, was taken over by Austria-Hungary in 1908, while Serbia, was an ally of Russia.

June 28
The Austrian Archduke is assassinated at Sarajevo.

August 1–4
War breaks out as Germany invades Belgium.

August 26–30
Germany inflicts a major defeat o the Russian forces at Tannenberg what is now Poland.

Great Britain and Ireland (from 1914)

Belgium (from 1914)

Canada (from 1914)

Newfoundland (from 1914)

Germany (from 1914)

Russia (from 1914 to 1917)

USA (from 1917)

France (from 1914)

Portugal (from 1916)

Austria-Hungary (from 1914)

Romania (from 1916)

Japan (from 1914)

Italy (from 1915)

Bulgaria (from 1915)

India (from 1914)

Montenegro and Serbia (from 1914)

Greece (from 1915)

Ottoman Empire (Turkey) (from 1914)

New Zealand (from 1914)

Australia (from 1914)

South Africa (from 1914)

Between 1914 and 1917 numerous countries across the globe were dragged into the conflict.

SARAJEVO 1914

On June 28, 1914, the heir to the throne of Austria-Hungary, Archduke Franz Ferdinand, was shot dead in Sarajevo, Bosnia. The assassin, Gavrilo Princip, wanted the Balkan states to unite as a single independent nation. The Austrians, encouraged by Germany, blamed Serbia. In August, the war began as Germany invaded Russia's ally, France. Germany had decided to invade France by way of its neutral neighbor, Belgium, before the massive Russian army was ready to attack in the east. Great Britain, in support of Belgium, joined the war against Germany. So did Japan, and from 1915 Italy, too (having switched sides). The Ottoman Empire sided with Germany, hoping to win back lands it had lost in the Balkans. The USA stayed neutral until 1917, when it too declared war on Germany.

BUILDING BATTLESHIPS

From 1898, Germany started to increase the size of its navy. In 1908, Great Britain, then the world's leading naval power, retaliated by building more – and more heavily armed – warships of its own, known as dreadnoughts, such as this one. During the war, these ships competed for dominance of the seas.

September 5–10
The German advance into France is halted at the Marne River leading to stalemate on the Western Front.

September 14–November 2
1st Battle of Ypres, Belgium.

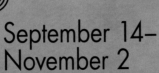

October 29
The Ottoman Empire joins the war on the side of the Central Powers.

IT'S WAR!

In August 1914, young men across Europe rushed to volunteer as soldiers. They thought the war would bring glory and adventure, and everyone was saying it would all be over 'by Christmas'. Newspapers and politicians on both sides whipped up patriotic pride and hatred of the enemy. Men who didn't volunteer or refused to fight were labelled as cowards.

GREAT BRITAIN

GERMANY

Western Front in 1916

FRANCE

Italian Front in 1916

ITALY

THE WESTERN FRONT

The German army's rapid advance into France almost reached Paris but was halted by French and British forces. The Germans were pushed back to the River Marne. Total casualties there numbered about 483,000. Both sides now dug in and soon a long network of trenches stretched from the English Channel to the Swiss border. The war on this Western Front would drag on for four years, with massive loss of life and little ground won or lost.

THE ITALIAN FRONT

Fierce battles were fought by Italian troops along Austria-Hungary's southern borders, along the mountain ranges of the Alps, the river valleys of Slovenia and the plains of Italy, Serbia and Macedonia.

In 1917, the USA, infuriated by German attacks on neutral shipping, joined the war in Western Europe.

US soldiers race towards the enemy in 1917.

British troops march across no-man's land in 1916.

1915

April 22– May 25
2nd Battle of Ypres, Belgium.

April 25
Allied troops land at Gallipoli, Turkey.

May 23
Italy changes alliance to join the Allied Powers.

RUSSIA

Eastern Front in 1916

THE EASTERN FRONT

Along the Eastern Front, the war was faster moving than in the west, but no less deadly. The Russians advanced on Germany but were halted by a massive defeat at Tannenberg. To the south, the troops of Austria-Hungary struggled to hold back the Russian forces.

By 1917, both sides were exhausted. The Austrians were trying to make peace, and in that same year Russian soldiers were deserting the front to join a revolution back home. The Tsar, the leader of Russia, was overthrown in March and a second revolution that November brought the Bolsheviks (radical communists) to power. They withdrew Russia from the war.

With their war nearing its end, Russian troops crouch in a trench awaiting a German attack in 1917.

German soldiers head into battle at the start of the war in August 1914.

1916

May 31– June 1
Naval battle of Jutland between German and British fleets.

July 1st– November 18
1st Battle of the Somme, France.

September 15
The first use of tanks in battle by the British army.

THE WIDER WAR

Troops from many lands served in World War I, including Indians, Gurkhas, Caribbeans, North Africans, Australians, New Zealanders, South Africans, Canadians and Japanese. In Africa, troops fought for their colonial rulers. There was military action in China and Africa and a naval battle off the Falkland Islands in the South Atlantic.

★ TECHNOLOGICAL WAR ★

This was a modern war fought in submarines under the sea and by airplanes and airships in the skies. On the ground, the defensive power of machine guns (above), barbed wire and high-explosive shells was too much for old-fashioned charges of soldiers to overcome. The result was years of stalemate, particularly on the Western Front.

Gallipoli

OTTOMAN EMPIRE

SOUTHWEST ASIA

The biggest area of conflict outside Europe was in southwest Asia, then ruled by the Ottoman Empire. In 1915–1916, the Allied powers decided to land troops on Turkey's Gallipoli peninsula in a bid to break through the Ottomans' defenses and open up a corridor to support the Russians. It was a terrible mistake which in total would cost about 500,000 casualties. In 1917, attention moved to the more oil-rich regions of what is now Iraq. Allied troops eventually captured Baghdad, but Turkish troops attacked the Suez Canal and there was bitter fighting for Palestine. The Allies supported the Arabs as they revolted against Turkish rule.

1917

March 15
Russia's leader, the Tsar, is overthrown.

April 6
The USA joins the Allied side as an Associate Power.

June 16– November 10
The Passchendaele offensive causes over 500,000 casualties.

November 7
Following a second revolution, Russia withdraws from the war.

HOW THE WAR ENDED

By 1917, all sides were suffering greatly, but the tide had begun to turn against the Central Powers. The arrival of fresh troops and supplies from the United States had given the Allies new hope. The 'Hundred Days' Offensive on the Western Front pushed the Germans into retreat. In September, Bulgaria signed an armistice agreement, followed by the Ottoman Empire in October. Austria-Hungary was defeated at Vittorio Veneto in northern Italy in early November. With communist uprisings taking place in Munich and Berlin, Germany, too, agreed to an armistice on November 11, The war was over.

A British general gives a speech to his troops following the capture of a German-held bridge in October, 1918.

WORLD WAR I FIGURES

NAME: PAUL VON HINDENBURG
LIVED: 1847–1934
JOB: CHIEF OF GERMAN GENERAL STAFF

Following several victories over Russia, Field Marshall Hindenburg became the head of the German army in 1916. With the Kaiser sidelined, this effectively made him Germany's leader. He remained popular even after Germany's defeat and would later serve as the country's democratic president.

"AT 11 O'CLOCK ON THE DAY ITSELF
A TRUMPETER CAME ROUND AND SOUNDED THE 'CEASE FIRE',
QUITE DRAMATICALLY.
I REMEMBER DOING A CARTWHEEL
AND I SAID TO MYSELF, 'I'M ALIVE!
IT'S ALL OVER AND I'M ALIVE!"

British Gunner G Worsley, Royal Field Artillery.

1918

August 8
The 100 Days offensive, which will eventually end the conflict begins on the Western Front.

November 3
The German fleet mutinies at Kiel.

November 11
The Allies and the Germans sign an Armistice.

The poppies that grew on the battlefields have become a symbol of the war.

AFTER THE WAR

British civilians cheer and clamber aboard a truck to celebrate victory in 1918.

Many Allied troops reacted to the Armistice with stunned silence. As the news sunk in, there was cheering along the lines. In the streets of London, Paris and New York huge crowds were soon singing and waving flags.

HEADING HOME

After the troops came home, there were joyful reunions, but also deep grief for those not returning, and anxiety about those who came back wounded, blinded or in a state of distress. In Germany, there was relief that the war was over, but also bitterness at defeat, severe shortages of food and violent political strife between Freikorps (militias run by former army officers) and communist rebels. To make matters even worse, an influenza pandemic raged around the world from 1918 to 1920, infecting about 500 million people, of whom more than 50 million died.

The so-called 'Big Four' of (left to right) David Lloyd George, Vittorio Orlando, Georges Clemenceau and Woodrow Wilson.

PEACE TREATIES

The armistice agreements ended the fighting, but the terms of the settlement were not decided until the Paris Peace Conference of 1919. The chief negotiators were French Prime Minister Georges Clemenceau, British Prime Minister David Lloyd George, Italian Prime Minster Vittorio Orlando and US President Woodrow Wilson. The defeated nations were not consulted – the terms were imposed rather than agreed. The conference produced five separate peace treaties, for Germany, Austria, Hungary, Bulgaria and Turkey.

TIMELINE OF THE PEACE

1919

The Paris Peace Conference ends with the signing of the Treaty of Versailles, confirming peace with Germany.

1919

The League of Nations is founded in Paris.

1921

Adolf Hitler becomes leader of the National Socialist German Workers' (Nazi) Party.

ESTONIA
LATVIA
LITHUANIA
GER.
RUSSIA
GREAT BRITAIN
GERMANY
POLAND
CZECHOSLOVAKIA
FRANCE
AUSTRIA HUNGARY
ROMANIA
YUGOSLAVIA
ITALY
BULGARIA
ALBANIA
GREECE
TURKEY

Borders 1914

RUSSIAN EMPIRE
GERMAN EMPIRE
AUSTRIA-HUNGARY
MONTENEGRO
SERBIA
OTTOMAN EMPIRE

As empires broke up, several new countries emerged after the war, including Austria, Hungary, Czechoslovakia and Turkey.

A NEW WORLD MAP

Germany became a democratic republic with its capital at Weimar. France took over the border region of Alsace and its troops occupied the Rhineland in western Germany. The map of Europe was redrawn, with the creation of a new nation called Czechoslovakia and a new Polish republic. Italy gained Austrian territory. The Ottoman Empire and Germany's overseas empire were broken up. The map of the world had changed greatly in just five years.

WORLD WAR I FIGURES ★

NAME: **KAISER WILHELM II**
LIVED: **1859–1941**
JOB: **GERMAN EMPEROR**

The aggressive policies of the emperor led his country into war. Sidelined by his generals during the conflict, he abdicated when Germany was defeated and spent the rest of his life in exile in the Netherlands.

1922
After five years of Civil War in Russia, the Soviet Union is founded.

1922
Fascists seize power in Italy.

1923
Hyperinflation sends the German economy into meltdown.

1929
The Wall Street Crash in the USA signals the start of the Great Depression.

A WAR TO END ALL WARS?

In 1914, the English writer H G Wells claimed that this would be 'the war that will end war'. He later regretted using these words. Another writer, George Santayana, added more realiztically, 'only the dead have seen the end of war'. Fighting continued around the world throughout the years after World War I, leading up to an even more terrible conflict, World War II (1939–1945).

The Russian Tsar, Nicholas II, was overthrown in 1917 and executed in 1918.

A JUST WAR?

Most people agree that World War I was an appalling tragedy. Some blame the loss of life on senior army officers, some on the politicians. Others believe that the horrors could not have been avoided, given the new forms of warfare. Nobody doubts the bravery of those who fought and died.

Many argued that the war was necessary to stop militarism and the rise of autocracy, a form of government in which one person holds all the power. Woodrow Wilson talked about 'making the world safe for democracy'. But neither sides were angels. The Ottoman Empire was an autocracy and the German head of state was the boastful, troubled Kaiser. But on the Allied side, Russia too was ruled by the autocratic Tsar Nicholas II.

"WHEN THE DAYS OF REJOICING ARE OVER, WHEN THE FLAGS ARE STOWED SAFELY AWAY, THEY WILL DREAM OF ANOTHER WILD 'WAR TO END WARS' AND ANOTHER WILD ARMISTICE DAY. BUT THE BOYS WHO WERE KILLED IN THE TRENCHES, WHO FOUGHT WITH NO RAGE AND NO RANT, WE LEFT THEM STRETCHED OUT ON THEIR PALLETS OF MUD LOW DOWN WITH THE WORM AND THE ANT."

Armistice Day, 1918, by the poet Robert Graves.

SOCIAL CHANGES

Women's rights campaigner urging women to vote in Britain after the war.

During the war, only 60 percent of British men could vote (compared with all males in Germany), and no women at all. The citizens of the British, French and German colonial empires and the Aborigines of Australia had neither votes nor civil rights. African American soldiers in the war were officially treated as inferior.

It could certainly be argued that the horrors of World War I started the move towards social change and progress towards democratic reforms, such as universal suffrage (votes for all men and women). The experience of service in the war also strengthened the calls for independence among the peoples of the European colonies.

Australian troops walk through a hellish landscape of shattered trees and muddy shell holes after the Passchendaele offensive, 1917.

★ FIRST WORLD WAR FIGURES ★

YOUR COUNTRY NEEDS "YOU"

NAME: **LORD KITCHENER**
LIVED: **1815–1916**
JOB: **BRITAIN'S SECRETARY OF STATE FOR WAR**

Herbert Kitchener was shown on a famous wartime poster, which was used to recruit soldiers. Unlike his colleagues in the British government, he always believed that the war would be a long one and would be won by the side with the greatest manpower. He died when HMS *Hampshire* struck a mine in 1916.

ENDING MILITARISM?

Far from seeing an end to war, the decades after World War I saw increased, rather than decreased, militarism. In Germany, the extremely militaristic Nazi Party came to power, fuelled by resentment of the harsh terms of the Treaty of Versailles. Militarism also took hold in the former Allied power of Japan and in fascist Italy.

WHAT PRICE PEACE?

Did Word War I leave the world a safer place? The Paris Peace Conference of 1919 was supposed to re-set international relations and begin healing the wounds of war. Many of the delegates, including the US President Woodrow Wilson, hoped it would do just that, but the outcome fell far short of their desires.

★ HYPERINFLATION ★

PAYBACK TIME

To bring about a lasting peace, it is always a good idea to talk to the losers as well as the winners. But the Germans were not asked to the conference. At the Paris talks, France demanded a financial paybacks known as reparations. Germany ended up being presented with a massive bill of $33 billion. In the years that followed, the German currency became almost worthless. When it became impossible to pay back any more, French troops occupied Germany's industrial heartland, the region of the Ruhr. In Germany, these harsh terms caused great anger, which helped the rise of the Nazis.

In 1923, German inflation spiralled out of control. A loaf of bread that cost 250 marks in January cost a staggering 200 million marks by November. Vast amounts of cash were printed to keep up with the rises (above). The crisis ended when a new currency was issued backed by an American loan.

French troops keep a lookout over the German Rhineland, which they occupied until 1930.

"DOESN'T THE WHOLE TROUBLE IN EUROPE TODAY GO BACK TO THE VERSAILLES TREATY, THAT INSTRUMENT OF PERFIDY AND DISHONOR?
... IT SEEMS TO ME THAT PRACTICALLY ALL OUR ILLS ARE DIRECTLY CHARGEABLE TO THE VERSAILLES TREATY."

US politician Harold L Ickes, 1923.

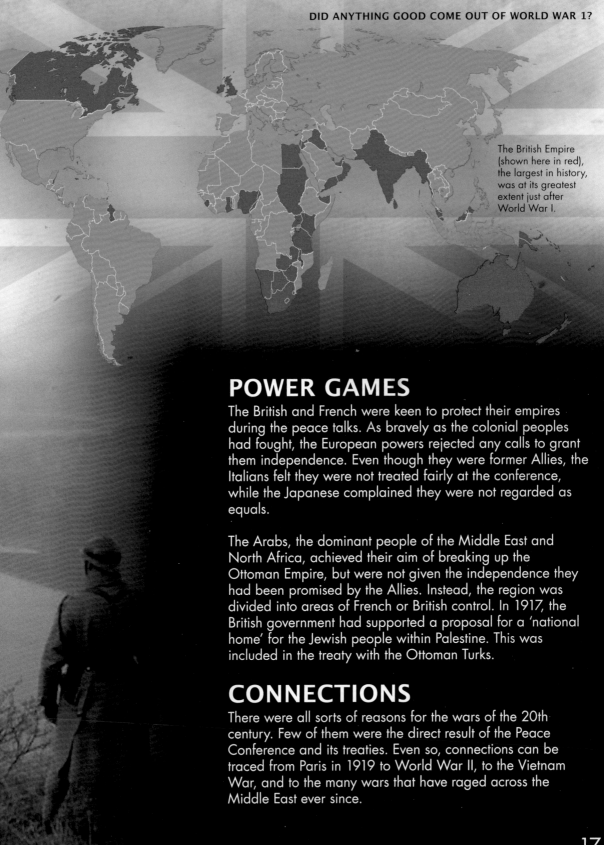

The British Empire (shown here in red), the largest in history, was at its greatest extent just after World War I.

POWER GAMES

The British and French were keen to protect their empires during the peace talks. As bravely as the colonial peoples had fought, the European powers rejected any calls to grant them independence. Even though they were former Allies, the Italians felt they were not treated fairly at the conference, while the Japanese complained they were not regarded as equals.

The Arabs, the dominant people of the Middle East and North Africa, achieved their aim of breaking up the Ottoman Empire, but were not given the independence they had been promised by the Allies. Instead, the region was divided into areas of French or British control. In 1917, the British government had supported a proposal for a 'national home' for the Jewish people within Palestine. This was included in the treaty with the Ottoman Turks.

CONNECTIONS

There were all sorts of reasons for the wars of the 20th century. Few of them were the direct result of the Peace Conference and its treaties. Even so, connections can be traced from Paris in 1919 to World War II, to the Vietnam War, and to the many wars that have raged across the Middle East ever since.

17

THE LEAGUE
OF NATIONS

The big plan at the Paris Peace Conference was to create a 'League of Nations'. This would be an international treaty organization which could prevent the rush to war that had happened in summer 1914. The League would discourage war through diplomacy, international law and disarmament.

HOW TO STOP NEW WARS

With the enthusiastic support of the French and British governments, and the US President Woodrow Wilson, the League of Nations came into being on January 1920. Based in Geneva, Switzerland, it lasted until 1946. It gave official permissions, called mandates, for the former Allied powers to govern the territories of the German and Ottoman empires. By 1935, the League had 58 member nations. It set up organizations for health and international labor, and commissions to deal with slavery, child labor, disarmament and refugees. It had many successes, such as sorting out border disputes and tackling the deadly trade in opium.

The League of Nations (below left) campaigned against child labor, such as the employment of children in mining (above).

"WE ARE PARTICIPANTS, WHETHER WE WOULD OR NOT, IN THE LIFE OF THE WORLD. THE INTERESTS OF ALL NATIONS ARE OURS ALSO. WE ARE PARTNERS WITH THE REST."

US President Woodrow Wilson, 1920.

ANOTHER FAILURE?

Sadly, the League's failures were big ones. It failed to prevent a new arms race. Japan invaded China in 1931, Italy invaded Abyssinia (Ethiopia) in 1935. The League of Nations stood by during the Spanish Civil War (1936–1939). Most importantly, it couldn't stop World War II. What had gone wrong? For a start, the world's most powerful nation had refused to join. Despite all Woodrow Wilson's hard work, the US Senate voted to stay out. It demanded to keep the right to go to war if and when it wanted. Other powerful member nations were not prepared to use their armies or bring in sanctions in support of the League's demands. The League lacked muscle.

The town of Guernica lies in ruins in 1937 at the height of the Spanish Civil War, a conflict the League was powerless to prevent.

★ THE ROAD TO THE UN ★

The League of Nations may have failed, but it was one of the most important ideas to come out of World War I. By 1943, the Allies in World War II were already planning a body to take the place of the League. By now, this kind of international cooperation was seen as essential.

With its distinctive white-on-blue emblem (left), the United Nations (UN), founded in 1945, was far more successful than the League. Although the UN today still has many critics and is limited in what it can do, it has 193 member nations and contributes to the world's health and welfare. Its Universal Declaration of Human Rights, which was adopted in 1948, was a response to the horrors of the two World Wars. It sets out the basic requirements for human freedom and justice.

THE RULES OF WAR

Australian troops in a trench wearing gas masks to protect them against gas attacks in 1917.

To the soldiers in the trenches, World War I often seemed like a chaotic nightmare, but it had its rules and laws. Throughout history, armies had fought according to agreements that dealt with the conduct of soldiers, how prisoners, spies and civilians should be treated, and with ceasefires and talks.

British casualties of a gas attack hold on to each other in 1918.

CREATING THE RULES

International codes of wartime conduct, known as the Hague Conventions, were in force during World War I. But they didn't cover many of the horrific new weapons. Deadly canisters of mustard gas, chlorine and phosgene were used on the battlefield by both sides. The results of gas poisoning included choking, blindness, blistering and death.

Lessons had been learned. After the war, chemical and biological weapons were partially banned under the Geneva Protocol of 1925. This paved the way for more strict laws, such as the Biological Weapons Convention of 1972. These were important and necessary steps in making the world a safer place.

THE RED CROSS

The International Committee of the Red Cross was founded in 1863 in Switzerland, to protect the victims of war, regardless of their nationality, their politics or their religious beliefs. During World War I, the Red Cross was transformed into a huge organization. Red Cross nurses from all over the world came to help in the hospitals of the countries at war. The organization set up an International Prisoner of War (PoW) Agency to look after the interests of captured soldiers. Red Cross officials also checked up on whether countries were obeying the Hague Conventions, and later helped bring about the Geneva Protocol on chemical weapons. Awarded the Nobel Peace Prize in 1917, the organization continued to be active after the war, working towards the protection of civilian populations by a Second Geneva Convention (1934).

The symbols of the Red Cross and Red Crescent are intended to protect the wearer against military attack.

Today, the International Federation of Red Cross and Red Crescent Socieites organizes international relief work during wars and other disasters all around the globe.

ROLES OF THE RED CROSS

During World War I, the Red Cross:
- Kept records of about 7 million soldiers missing in action or taken captive.
- Sent 1.9 million parcels of food and supplies to PoWs.
- Forwarded about 20 million personal letters and messages to PoWs.
- Transferred money worth about 18 million Swiss francs to PoWs.
- Arranged about 200,000 prisoner exchanges.
- Inspected conditions at 524 PoW camps in Europe.
- Organized the return of about 420,000 PoWs to their home countries when the war ended.

LIVES FIT FOR HEROES?

A poor US mother and her children during the Great Depression of the 1930s.

When the soldiers returned from the trenches, they found that many changes had taken place at home. Were these social changes for the better or the worse? Were they rewarded for their sacrifice?

THE GLOBAL ECONOMY

Faced with huge reparations, Germany's economy collapsed after the war. But the victors, Britain and France, were also struggling financially having run up enormous wartime expenses.

Soldiers returned home to face severe economic problems. By 1922, 1.5 million Britons were unemployed. Wages were reduced and in 1926 there was a general strike across Britain. Across the Atlantic, the US profited from sales and loans to Europe in the war, leading to a boom in the 1920s. But in 1929 the stock market collapsed in the Wall Street Crash, creating a global depression.

WORLD WAR I: THE BIG SPENDERS

●●●●●●●●●●●●●●●●●●●●●●●●●●●●●●●●●●●●●●● Germany 37,775,000,000

●●●●●●●●●●●●●●●●●●●●●●●●●●●●●●●●●●●● Great Britain 35,334,012,000

●●●●●●●●●●●●●●●●●●●●●●●●●●●●● France 24,265,583,000

●●●●●●●●●●●●●●●●●●●●●●●●●● USA 22,625,253,000

●●●●●●●●●●●●●●●●●●●●●●●●●● Russia 22,293,950,000

● = US$ 1 million   ●●●●●●●●●●●●●●●●●●●●●●● Austria-Hungary 20,622,960,000

"WHAT IS OUR TASK? TO MAKE BRITAIN A LAND FIT FOR HEROES TO LIVE IN."

British Prime Minster David Lloyd George, November 24, 1918.

A crowd of protesters gathers outside a US bank which collapsed after the Wall Street Crash.

SOCIAL CHANGES

These economic earthquakes shook up the social order. The right for everybody to vote could be held back no longer. New political parties grew up to represent the working class, the poor and the unemployed.

There was a change too in the way governments dealt with social and economic problems. During the war, populations had become more used to centralized planning by the state. For the next 60 years, many European governments took on more responsibilities to care for their citizens, building homes and creating a welfare state with healthcare and other benefits paid for by taxation. In the USA, a political program known as the New Deal relied on central government projects to beat the depression from 1933–1938.

Young workers employed by the US government construct a road as part of the New Deal.

★ WORLD WAR I FIGURES ★

NAME: **DAVID LLOYD GEORGE**
LIVED: **1863–1945**
JOB: **BRITISH PRIME MINISTER**

Lloyd George began the war as Britain's Minister of Munitions, overseeing the construction and supply of weapons. But following the disasters at Gallipoli and the Somme, and the stalemate on the Western Front, he replaced the unpopular Prime Minister Herbert Asquith in 1916. He held this position until 1922, acting as Britain's chief negotiator at the Paris peace talks.

HEALTH AND MEDICINE

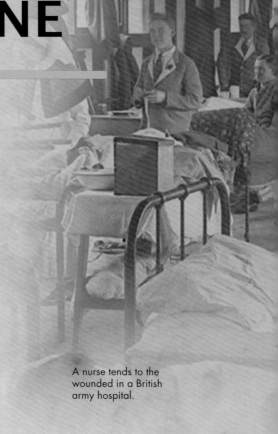

The armaments of Word War I caused more casualties than the weapons of any previous war. Common health problems in the flooded, rat-infested trenches included severe wounds, gangrene, concussion, typhus, dysentery and trenchfoot. Amputation of limbs was often necessary.

NEW LIVE SAVERS

Out of this tragic suffering came many medical advances, which went on to benefit society as a whole. New types of splint were developed to help broken bones mend, while the introduction of motor ambulances and hospital trains helped the sick and injured receive medical treatment quicker. Hospital emergency treatment improved and public health officials learned valuable lessons from both world wars.

A nurse tends to the wounded in a British army hospital.

★ ANTISEPTICS

Infection-fighting antibiotics had not yet been discovered, but antiseptics were much improved during the war. A chemical solution called the Carrel-Dakin treatment was invented by British chemist Henry Drydale Dakin and French surgeon Alexis Carrel and used for the first time during the conflict. It worked much better than earlier germ killers, such as iodine or carbolic acid.

★ BLOOD TRANSFUSIONS

Blood transfusion was another great wartime lifesaver. The first indirect blood transfusion using stored blood (rather than blood given directly from one patient to another) was carried out just before the conflict. The practice became widespread on the Western Front where the world's first blood banks were also established. After the war, blood donation and storage became much more common.

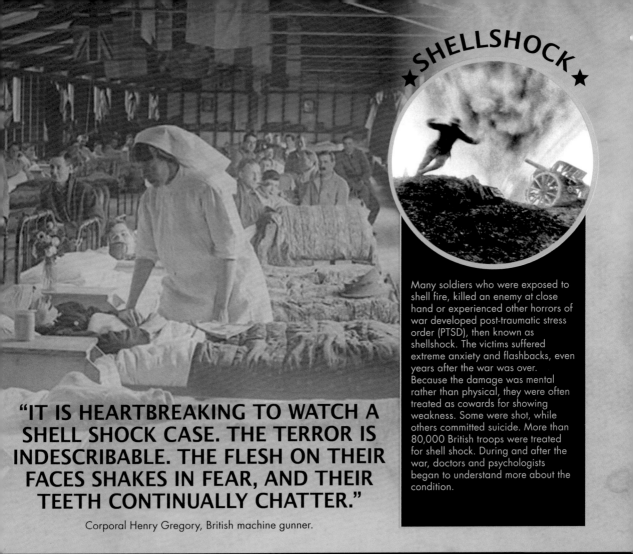

Many soldiers who were exposed to shell fire, killed an enemy at close hand or experienced other horrors of war developed post-traumatic stress order (PTSD), then known as shellshock. The victims suffered extreme anxiety and flashbacks, even years after the war was over. Because the damage was mental rather than physical, they were often treated as cowards for showing weakness. Some were shot, while others committed suicide. More than 80,000 British troops were treated for shell shock. During and after the war, doctors and psychologists began to understand more about the condition.

"IT IS HEARTBREAKING TO WATCH A SHELL SHOCK CASE. THE TERROR IS INDESCRIBABLE. THE FLESH ON THEIR FACES SHAKES IN FEAR, AND THEIR TEETH CONTINUALLY CHATTER."

Corporal Henry Gregory, British machine gunner.

★ X–RAYS

The medical use of X-rays was being developed at this time, too. The Nobel Prize winning Polish scientist Marie Sklodowska-Curie (below) helped to pioneer the use of X-rays in surgery. During the war, she had cars fitted with the equipment, and drove them herself from Paris all the way to the Western Front where she took X-rays of wounded soldiers.

Marie Curie was head of radiology for the International Red Cross.

★ PLASTIC SURGERY

Shrapnel wounds could cause terrible damage to the head and face. New Zealand-born Dr Harold Gillies was the father of plastic surgery, developing his techniques at The Queen's Hospital in Sidcup, England. The first patient was the sailor Walter Yeo (seen here) who received a facial skin graft after he was injured at the naval Battle of Jutland in 1916. Over 5,000 men were treated at the hospital.

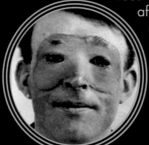

WOMEN'S RIGHTS

"YOU ARE DOING A MAN'S WORK AND SO YOU ARE DRESSED RATHER LIKE A MAN; BUT REMEMBER THAT BECAUSE YOU WEAR A SMOCK AND TROUSERS YOU SHOULD TAKE CARE TO BEHAVE LIKE AN ENGLISH GIRL WHO EXPECTS CHIVALRY AND RESPECT FROM EVERYONE SHE MEETS".

Guidelines for members of the Women's Land Army.

Long before the war, women had been campaigning for equal rights, especially for suffrage – the right to vote. The first nation to give women the right to vote in a general election was New Zealand in 1893. In Britain, the radical Women's Social and Political Union was founded in 1903. These 'Suffragettes' took direct action and many went to prison for their beliefs. They suspended their campaign when the war broke out.

WOMEN AT WAR

As the men marched off to fight, women moved into jobs that only men had done before. They learned to drive motor ambulances. They became bus conductors. They worked in munitions factories and coal mines. Some became school teachers or worked in offices. In Germany, women came to make up 37 percent of the workforce. In the USA, women were given back-up jobs in the armed services.

In Britain too, a Women's Army Auxiliary Corps (WAAC) was formed. These women served in France as cooks, mechanics and typists, but they did not receive equal pay with the men. On the Eastern Front, Russia formed Women's Battalions, which fought in combat. In the Ottoman Empire too, Turkish women fought as snipers.

FEEDING THE NATION

In Britain, a Women's 'Land Army' (WLA) was founded in 1915 – not to fight, but to get young women working on farms (as below) and producing vital food crops. By the end of 1917, an extra 250,000 women were working on farms. In 1915, a new enterprise was imported to Britain from Canada – the 'Women's Institute' (WI). This encouraged women to grow and preserve their own food. The WI is still a popular organizer of women's activities today.

★ WOMEN'S SUFFRAGE ★

Before the war, the Suffragettes and other campaigners for women's rights made many sacrifices for their beliefs – this image shows the leader of the Suffragette leader Emmeline Pankhurst being arrested . However, their huge contribution to the war effort convinced many politicians, on both the winning and losing sides, that it was finally time to give women the vote. There could be no going back to the pre-war days.

AFTER THE WAR

In Great Britain, the Sex Disqualification (Removal) Act of 1919, made it illegal for anyone to be refused work because they were a woman. However other laws ensured that men could return to many of their pre-war jobs. After the war, women over 30 could vote, but it was 1928 before men and women could both vote at 21.

Votes for Women Introduced

Country	Year
Canada	1917
Austria, Germany and Russia	1918
USA	1920
Great Britain and Ireland	1928
Turkey	1934

CHANGING DRESS

To meet the needs of working women, clothes became simpler and more useful during the war years. Corsets were not practical. The large hats of 1914 were replaced with smaller ones. Dresses and skirts had shorter hems and were looser. Some women even wore trousers or greatcoats in the style of the WAAC or WLA.

In the war, women began taking on jobs previously reserved for men, as shown by these female police officers in 1916.

SORROW AND JOY

People responded to the grief and horror of the war in different ways. Some raised funds for the care of wounded soldiers, while many local communities built war memorials to commemorate the dead, and organized services of remembrance. The participating nations also began building large cemeteries near the battlefields. These are still spread across the landscape today, a moving and grim reminder of the war.

PEACE CAMPAIGNS

Many people were determined to prevent such a war ever happening again. They threw themselves into political activity, inspiring an international interest in pacifism between the wars. The International Congress of Women took place in 1915 (left) leading to the foundation of the Women's International League for Peace and Freedom the same year, followed by the Peace Pledge Union in 1934.

WORLD WAR I FIGURES

NAME: **WOODROW WILSON**
LIVED: **1856–1924**
JOB: **US PRESIDENT**

To begin with, Wilson was a fierce opponent of the US joining the war. But he changed his mind when German U-boats began sinking American ships. He also supported the League of Nations, but couldn't persuade the US Congress to join . He was awarded the Nobel Peace Prize in 1919.

1914   1918

GLORIOUS MEMORY OF TH
WN WHO FEL N THE GR
NAM   EVER

THE PLEASURE SEEKERS

In Europe, many people just wanted to forget their wartime troubles and the hard times they were now experiencing. Spectator sports, such as soccer, attracted huge crowds. New technologies brought speed to sports such as motor racing and flying. Through the 1920s and 30s, motor transport, public and private (such as this motor car), transformed lives in the city and the countryside.

THE ROARING TWENTIES

The radio (or 'wireless') now broadcast into homes, while portable record players ('phonographs') could play the latest dance and jazz music. Hollywood and European studios offered glimpses of a glamorous world of film stars. The fashion revolution which had started in the war years became even more extreme. Women wore short dresses and make up, cut their hair short, drank alcohol and smoked cigarettes. These years would become known as the 'Roaring Twenties'. This new, frantic, youth culture, which the older generation often found shocking, could be seen as a reaction against the war years. Perhaps it seemed important to grasp the moment before another war came and destroyed the peace.

Fashionable young women of the 1920s, known as 'flappers', perform a popular dance known as the Charleston.

NEW TECHNOLOGIES

The desperation of war often drives scientists and engineers to make new discoveries. World War I produced tanks, poison gases, flamethrowers, new aircraft and submarines. Innovations like these were of great military use and helped the war effort, but as methods of killing and destruction they can hardly be seen as advances for mankind.

★ MASS PRODUCTION ★

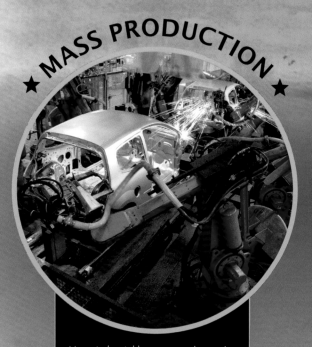

Many industrial lessons were learned during the war years. The American motor company, Ford, delivered 390,000 trucks to the US army in 1917. After the war, mass production of cars was the key to Ford's fantastic success, with 2 million Model T cars being produced in just one year, 1925.

★ TIRES

Before the war, German and Russian scientists had developed synthetic forms of rubber. Because international trade was disrupted by the war, there was soon a great shortage of natural rubber, which was grown in tropical regions of the world. Synthetic rubber for tires could now be made in factories on a large scale. The price of natural rubber was very high after World War I, so synthetic rubber continued to be made. By World War II, it could be produced very cheaply. It was later used in printing on textiles and as a solid fuel for rockets.

★ MAKING TRACKS

Although these were not a new invention, caterpillar tracks were developed and improved for tanks, which first appeared during the conflict in 1915. They were subsequently used in vehicles for agriculture and civil engineering purposes and, indeed, anywhere that involved working on rough terrain.

Unlike modern tanks, which have moving gun turrets on top, the guns in early tanks poked out of the sides of the vehicle.

★ RADIO ON THE MOVE

At the start of the war, telegraph communications were sent via cable, which often had to be laid through areas that were under fire. It was dangerous, exhausting work, and the messages could be intercepted easily by the enemy. Wireless radios overcame many of these problems. The first sets were very heavy, but mobile communications on the battlefield were the start of a wider telecommunications revolution that is still going on today.

★ GAS MASKS

Deadly technology is often matched by counter-inventions, designed to offer protection. The first large-scale use of poison gas on the battlefield took place in 1915. In the same year, a Russian chemist named Nikolay Zelinsky invented a gas mask (right) which contained a type of charcoal filter called activated carbon. This was full of tiny holes that could soak up the gases – and save lives.

SEA TO AIR

In order to give their troops a crucial edge in battle, each side tried to ensure they had the latest, fastest and most powerful equipment available. This led to rapid advances in transport technology, seeing the creation of giant aircraft-carrying ships and mobile, deadly planes mounted with machine guns.

One of the earliest aircraft carriers, HMS *Furious* was painted with 'Dazzle' camouflage to confuse enemy craft.

★ AIRSHIPS

The Germans built airships, known as 'Zeppelins', for aerial reconnaissance and bombing raids during the war. Afterwards, they developed a fleet of new airships in the hope of establishing an international air travel industry. But in 1937, the luxurious *Hindenburg* Zeppelin caught fire in New Jersey, killing 37 people. This accident, plus the development of long-haul aircraft, put an end to commercial airship travel.

★ AIRCRAFT CARRIERS

Ships could be built (or adapted) to carry aircraft. One of the first aircraft carriers was the British HMS *Ark Royal*, which had a flat deck added to it where aircraft could take off and land. Being able to land on moving ships was useful in war, but would also prove valuable in peacetime, for exploration and rescue missions.

A British pilot attempts to land his biplane on the deck of HMS *Furious*.

★ AIR TRAFFIC CONTROL

The use of radio was extended to aircraft in World War I. Pilots could locate enemy targets, and then direct artillery fire towards them, by sending radio signals in Morse code. Many pilots found the heavy radio sets slowed down the aircraft too much, though, and ditched them. Without ground-to-air radio communication, there would have been no modern aviation and no air-traffic control.

The famous German fighter pilot, the 'Red Baron' flew in a triplane.

The British used biplanes, like this SE5, during the war.

The lack of wing struts made the Junkers J-1 very aerodynamic.

One of the world's largest airships, the *Hindenburg* was named after Germany's military leader in World War I.

★ AIRCRAFT DESIGNS

Most of the aircraft used in World War I were biplanes (with two wing-stacks) or triplanes (with three). But the future direction of aviation was shown by the introduction of the first all-metal monoplane (a single-winger), the German Junkers J-1 in 1915. It was nicknamed the *Blechesel* ('tin donkey'). The war also saw the invention of interrupter gear for aircraft (right). This synchronized the firing of the gun with the action of the propeller, so that the pilot could fire straight ahead through the whirling blades.

★ UNDER THE OCEAN ★

Germany's fleet was successfully blockaded by the British navy in World War I, but German submarines known as U-boats hunted the Atlantic shipping which supplied the Allies. Between 1914 and 1918, these submerged killers sank nearly 5,000 ships. The fact that the Allies had no way of detecting the submarines kept the losses high. However, towards the end of the war, underwater listening devices, or hydrophones, were invented. They could detect U-boats as they moved around beneath the ocean's surface.

★ PARACHUTES

Although parachutes had been invented by the time war broke out, they were used only from stationary observation balloons at first. Inside the tiny cockpit of a biplane, there was little room for a bulky parachute. By 1918, both German and British pilots were using parachutes activated by rip-cords, but they were not yet reliable and accidents were common. When designs and techniques improved, parachutes would become an emergency lifeline for pilots all over the world.

DAILY LIFE

Many of the discoveries and advances made during the war turned out to have uses in peacetime too. The desire, on both sides, to make the soldier's life as simple and straightforward as possible inspired many innovations for eating, telling the time and dressing that would influence people's everyday lives once the conflict was over.

The Germans supplied their troops with tea bags, which had been invented in the USA in 1908.

★ TIME KEEPING

The war had some unexpected spin-offs and set new fashions. Before the war, most men carried pocket watches, often attached to their jacket or waistcoat by a small chain. These were not very practical in the crowded trenches, where timing was all important. Wristwatches were much easier to glance at quickly. They had been invented before the war, but now suddenly became very popular. They were often given as special presents and stayed in fashion for men and women throughout the 20th century.

An early wristwatch, as worn by US troops in World War I.

★ FOOD AND NUTRITION

For the first time in a war, frozen food was shipped to the armies, thawing on its way to the front. The troops' food on the front line often tasted horrible. British soldiers mostly ate tinned stew, tinned salted beef (known as bully beef) and very hard biscuits, which they would soften by dunking them in their mugs of tea. Tea could be used to disguise the taste of foul water (a source of disease), and to keep the soldiers warm.

It was in the war years that the practice of changing the clocks to 'summer time' or 'daylight saving time' was first introduced, as a way of saving the fuel needed for heating and lighting. This had been discussed for many years, but Germany and Austria-Hungary at last brought it in during 1916, and most other northern nations soon followed.

★ DAYLIGHT SAVING ★

VICTORY!
CONGRESS PASSES DAYLIGHT SAVING BILL

"Get Your Hoe Ready!"

★VITAMIN DEFICIENCIES

Poor diet sometimes left the troops short of vitamins, while back home, food shortages made malnutrition increasingly common. Britain was forced to bring in food rationing in 1918. In the cities of Germany, the Allied blockade meant that supplies were even more scarce. Many children suffered from rickets, a disease of the bones caused by a lack of calcium. A Berlin doctor named Kurt Huldschinsky discovered that a sun lamp, using ultraviolet rays, could help cure this condition.

★STAINLESS STEEL

Some technical developments of this period – such as adding chrome to the steel used for gun barrels – had non-military uses too. This 'stainless steel' was used to make knives and forks which did not rust or need polishing. It was ideal for surgical instruments too.

Wartime stainless steel technology is still used for making cutlery today.

★ZIP IT UP!

The zip fastener was invented in the USA as early as 1851, but the modern form of the zip, which has oval 'scoops' linked by a slider, did not make its first appearance until 1913. When America entered the war in 1917, zips were used by the US Navy and by airmen for their flying suits. The zip went on to become a popular replacement for buttons on civilian clothing in the 1920s, when its US name 'zipper' came into use. Today, we use lightweight zippers on everything from jackets and shoes to wallets.

WORLD WAR I FIGURES

NAME: **KONRAD ADENAUER**
LIVED: **1876–1967**
JOB: **MAYOR OF COLOGNE**

Adenauer was mayor of the German city of Cologne in 1917–1918. When supplies of meat ran out, he tried to solve the problem by inventing a non-meat sausage made of soya, maize, barley and rice. It didn't prove very popular at the time, but today's supermarkets sell lots of vegetarian sausages. Adenauer is better remembered as the Chancellor of West Germany from 1949–1963, when he led his country out of the ruins of World War II.

MEDIA AND THE ARTS

In all wars, there is a conflict of interests. On the one hand there is the right of the public to know what is being done in its name, and the right of journalists to criticize military or government policy. On the other hand, national security and the safety of the troops must be protected. The governments of World War I did their best to keep a tight control on the flow of information. Free speech was not a legacy of this war.

> "IF PEOPLE REALLY KNEW [THE TRUTH], THE WAR WOULD BE STOPPED TOMORROW. BUT OF COURSE THEY DON'T KNOW AND CAN'T KNOW."
>
> David Lloyd George, British Prime Minister, speaking to CP Scott, editor of the *Manchester Guardian*.

NEW MEDIA

The new art of the cinema was very popular, and governments quickly realized that 'picture palaces' were the ideal places for spreading official propaganda and stirring up patriotic feelings. The British government hoped films would help bring the USA into the war on its side.

The first ever public radio broadcast took place in New York in 1910, but radio had not yet reached a mass audience, and it was mostly shut down during the war. Britain's first public broadcast was not until 1920.

The American director D W Griffiths (right, wearing a bow tie) oversees the production of an anti-German film, 'Hearts of the World' (left), in a trench on the Western Front.

A 1915 propaganda poster urging British men to volunteer for combat.

PRESS PROPAGANDA

Most people learned about the war from newspapers. British newspapers published fake stories about atrocities alongside real news stories to stoke anti-German hatred. The British Defense of the Realm Act of 1914 (DORA) allowed little criticism of the war effort. In Germany, the military censored all articles.

At first no British reporters were allowed to visit the war zone. In the end, a small number were given permission to report from the front. The British public were told little of the mass slaughter on the Somme in 1916. Letters home from the troops were censored too, but by 1917 members of the public were beginning to put together a more realistic version of events.

In this German propaganda poster, a soldier is shown asking the public for help with the war effort.

Some British troops did produce their own little newspaper. *The Wipers Times* (left) was published from 1916 to 1918 ('Wipers' was the slang name for the Belgian town of Ypres). It was produced on a printing press that some soldiers had found abandoned. It was not full of serious articles, but did make fun of the daily chores and routines, and included verses and jokes to cheer up the troops. It gives us a more realiztic view of the war than many of the big newspapers.

MUSIC HALL AND THE WAR

A magician entertains the audience at a music hall performance in Britain.

At the start of the war the most popular entertainment in Britain was music hall. This was a live stage show featuring songs, comedy routines and magic tricks. The American version was called 'vaudeville', and in France and Germany 'cabarets' offered a similar mix of variety acts in clubs, bars and small theaters. In Britain, the music halls were used to recruit troops, with men from the audience being asked by the performers to step up and volunteer for the armed forces.

POPULAR SONGS

The patriotic and sentimental tunes of the music hall were the pop songs of the day. They were sung by troops marching off to the front line, or played on pianos in bars and parlors back home. Songs like 'It's a Long, Long Way to Tipperary' (1912), 'Keep the Home Fires Burning' (1914), or 'Pack up Your Troubles in your Old Kitbag' (1915) remain known today. 'Over There' (1917) was an American propaganda song which aimed to get men to enlist for the war in Europe.

The troops took up these songs, as well as traditional folk tunes and the hymns they sang on Sundays, and made up new words for them. Australian troops sang 'Who'll come a fighting the Kaiser with me?' to the tune of 'Waltzing Matilda'.

The slogan of this 1915 British propaganda poster was turned into a popular music hall song.

TWISTING LANGUAGE

Lots of songs included jokey versions of the French words that English soldiers heard on the street. These included: 'parlyvoo' (parlez-vous, 'do you speak?') 'san fairy ann' (ça ne fait rien, 'it doesn't matter') 'napoo' (il n'y a plus, 'there's no more').

> ## "PACK UP YOUR TROUBLES IN YOUR OLD KIT–BAG, AND SMILE, SMILE, SMILE."
>
> George Henry Powell and Felix Powell, 1915.

Charlie Chaplin is shown in full military gear in the poster for the film *Shoulder Arms*.

CHARLIE

Charlie Chaplin, a comic from the London music halls, moved to Hollywood in 1912, and during the war years he became one the most famous men in the world. He was criticized by the newspapers and politicians for not serving in the army, but he was loved by the troops. His films were shown in hospital wards to cheer up the injured soldiers – a valuable service in itself. In his 1918 film *Shoulder Arms* soldier Charlie disguises himself as a tree and captures the Kaiser. Chaplin had a lasting dislike of war. He thought that patriotism was 'the greatest insanity' and in 1932 he forecast that it would cause another war.

In the 1925 film, the *Gold Rush*, a starving Chaplin boils and eats his own shoes.

ARTS AND THE WAR

The experience of the war inspired many great works of art. The people who lived through World War I, and especially those who fought in it, went through extreme emotions including patriotism, pride, fear, horror, sorrow and anger. Many expressed these passions in their diaries and letters. Others wrote poetry, novels or plays, painted or drew pictures, or composed music.

WORDS FOR WAR AND PEACE

Many young poets died of disease or were killed in action during the war. The great poet Wilfred Owen was killed just a week before the Armistice. Nine of his poems were included in *War Requiem* (1962), one of the best known works of the English composer Benjamin Britten. The Canadian poet John McCrae died of pneumonia in 1918. His poem *In Flanders Field* became one of the most famous from the war. The Austrian poet Georg Trakl served with a medical unit on the Eastern Front, but in desperation took his own life in November 1914.

Some authors wrote accounts of their wartime experiences, such as *Testament of Youth* by the British nurse Vera Brittain. She became a pacifist and keen supporter of the League of Nations. The German writer Erich Maria Remarque wrote a novel called *Im Westen Nichts Neues* – 'All Quiet on the Western Front' (1928). It sold millions of copies worldwide and was made into a famous film.

Poster for the 1930 film of *All Quiet on the Western Front.*

"MY SUBJECT IS WAR AND THE PITY OF WAR. THE POETRY IS IN THE PITY."

Wilfred Owen wrote these words for a book of poems he hoped to publish in 1919. He died on November 4, 1918.

HAUNTING IMAGES

British artists were sent to record the war and produced memorable images of the men and the devastation. Paul Nash's 1918 painting, showing tree stumps, craters and mud, has the title 'We Are Making a New World'. The German artist Otto Dix served on both the Western and the Eastern Front between 1915 and 1918. He was haunted by nightmares of his experiences, and in 1924 published 50 etchings, called

The devastation of a bombardment on the Western Front is captured by the British war artist Paul Nash in his 1918 painting 'The Mule Track'.

THE BIG QUESTIONS

Can war ever bring benefits to humanity? Militarists believe that war teaches discipline, duty and patriotic values. Pacifists disagree. They believe that warfare brutalizes people and that violence only brings about more violence. Many religions forbid all killing and call for non-violence. Some socialists refused to fight in World War I because they believed that this was no more than a power struggle to benefit the ruling classes. They claimed that ordinary people were just being used as 'cannon fodder'.

LOSS OF LIFE

World War I was one of the deadliest conflicts in history. Some 17 million people died while another 20 million were wounded. But what did this mass slaughter achieve? For the most part, the good things that did come out of World War I were not the original aims of either side back in 1914. They included laws and new organizations to make good the damage done by the war, or to prevent it happening again. They included responses to the war, such as poetry, paintings and films, as well as medical advances. The war also hastened social changes that would probably have taken place anyway, but at a slower pace. Did any of these outcomes justify the carnage?

"I FELT THEN, AS I FEEL NOW, THAT THE POLITICIANS WHO TOOK US TO WAR SHOULD HAVE BEEN GIVEN THE GUNS AND TOLD TO SETTLE THEIR DIFFERENCES THEMSELVES, INSTEAD OF ORGANIZING NOTHING BETTER THAN LEGALIZED MASS MURDER."

Harry Patch (1898–2009), the last surviving British soldier of World War I.

Members of the German Nazi party wear armbands bearing its symbol, the swastika, at a rally in 1932.

THE RISE OF POLITICAL EXTREMISM

Many of the nations that fought in World War I were ruled by monarchies. Most were replaced after the conflict by new forms of government. The emperors of Germany and Austria-Hungary, as well as the Sultan of the Ottoman Empire, were forced to abdicate. In Russia, the Tsar was executed and a communist regime took over. As the economic problems of the Great Depression spread around the world in the 1930s, people began looking for politically extreme solutions. In Italy, the fascists of Mussolini were in power, while Germany came to be dominated by the Nazis of Adolf Hitler. His plans for German expansion would draw the world into an even more deadly conflict between 1939 and 1945.

★ WORLD WAR I FIGURES ★

NAME: ADOLF HITLER

LIVED: 1889–1945

JOB: SOLDIER ON THE WESTERN FRONT

Hitler's experiences as a soldier in World War I had a major effect on his later career. He felt Germany had been humiliated and became determined to make it a powerful nation again. As the leader of the Nazi party, he seized power in 1933, turning Germany from a democracy into a fascist state heading for war.

43

POSITIVE EFFECTS OF WORLD WAR I

Was there really a silver lining to the events of 1914, or were there just dark clouds, the beginnings of a great storm which would continue to rattle the windows long after the war ended in 1918?

★ INTERNATIONAL RELATIONS

One lasting benefit to come out of the conflict was the creation of international bodies to try and resolve disputes between nations, first with the League of Nations and later (and more successfully) with the United Nations. However, combat in the 21st century is often called 'asymmetric', or unbalanced. Armies no longer line up against each other in trench warfare. Official armies often fight unofficial armies and militias who do not represent nations and have not signed international treaties. Both official and unofficial armies may ignore Geneva Conventions and resort to the tactics of terrorism. Fortunately, another body founded just after war, in 1919, the International Red Cross, is still helping those caught up in conflicts.

An armored personnel carrier being driven by United Nations peacekeeping troops.

★TECHNOLOGICAL IMPROVEMENTS

As with most wars, World War I saw the introduction of numerous new military technologies, such as tanks, as well as new types of ship and aircraft. But there were also other more peaceful innovations that made the transition from wartime to peace time. These included radio technology, caterpillar tracks, parachutes, tea bags, wrist watches and zippers (left).

★CULTURE

Some of the most powerful art of the 20th century was created as a result of World War I. The stories, poems, paintings, sculptures and music inspired by the conflict were the artists' way of trying to make sense of the immense human tragedy. Permanent memorials to the bravery and sacrifice of the soldiers, such as the Menin Gate in Belgium (left), were also erected.

"THERE'S A SILVER LINING, THROUGH THE DARK CLOUDS SHINING, TURN THE DARK CLOUD INSIDE OUT 'TIL THE BOYS COME HOME."

These were the words of the popular 1914 song 'Keep the Home-Fires Burning', by Ivor Novello and Lena Gilbert Ford.

As the poppy was one of the first flowers to grow again in the disturbed, churned-up earth of no-man's land, it was adopted as a symbol of the war in the 1920s.

GLOSSARY

abdicate
To give up the throne and stop ruling.

airship
A gas-filled aircraft which can be steered and self-propelled

allies
Nations that are on the same side.

antiseptic
Killing germs.

armistice
An agreement to end combat, before a treaty is signed,

assassin
Someone who murders, for politics or for pay.

autocracy
Rule by a monarch with unlimited powers.

colony
A territory which is ruled or settled by another country.

communism
A political system based upon public ownership and government by a party claiming to represent the workers.

dazzle camouflage
Bright colors used to break up the outline of an object, making it more difficult to see.

democratic
Based upon a system of government by the people.

diplomacy
Carrying out negotiations.

dugout
A military position dug from the soil and used for shelter or firing guns.

empire
A state made up of various territories ruled by one country.

fascism
A political system based on extreme nationalism and militarism.

gangrene
The dying off of living tissue, through a lack of blood circulation.

inflation
An increase in the price of goods and services.

malnutrition
A lack of enough good food to keep the body in health.

mandate
A commission for one country to govern another.

militarism
Glorification of the armed services and warfare.

militia
An irregular armed force, as opposed to a national army.

munitions
Materials used for war, such as weapons and ammunition.

neutral
Not taking sides.

no-man's land
The disputed area between two battling armies.

offensive
A major strategic attack across a broad area.

pandemic
Describes a disease that spreads across an entire region or the whole world.

propaganda
Information, often distorted or untrue, intended to harm or help a cause.

reconnaissance
Gaining information about the enemy.

reparation
Compensation, making amends.

republic
A country ruled by representatives of the people.

shellshock
Nervous reaction to stress or shock.

shrapnel
Metal fragments or bullets scattered by an explosion.

suffrage
The right to vote.

transfusion
The transfer of new blood into a body.

U-boat
A German submarine.

welfare state
A state which provides assistance to the old, sick, disabled or unemployed.

FOR MORE INFORMATION

★ BOOKS TO READ

Documenting History: World War I
Philip Steele
Wayland (2014)
An account of World War I, backed by quotations, newspaper articles, speeches, diaries and paintings.

Men, Women and Children: In the First World War
Philip Steele
Wayland (2013)
Life on the Home Front, food, dress and schooling.

Eyewitness: World War I
Simon Adams
Dorling Kindersley (2014)
A guide to the war, through fascinating visual images.

The Story of the First World War for Children
John Malam
Carlton Books (2014)
A wide ranging introduction to the Great War.

★ MUSEUMS AND WEBSITES TO VISIT

Imperial War Museum London
Lambeth Road
London SE17 6HZ
www.iwm.org.uk/visits/iwm-london
First World War Galleries telling moving stories from the war and from the Home Front.

National WWI Museaum and Memorial
100 W. 26th St.
Kansas City, MO 64108
(816) 888-8100
Website: https://theworldwar.org
Home to one of the largest Great War collections in the world--more than 75,000 items strong--the National WWI Museum is the official World War I museum of the United States.

WEBSITES
Because of the changing nature of Internet links, Rosen Publishing has developed an online list of websites related to the subject of this book. This site is updated regularly. Please use this link to access this list:

http://www.rosenlinks.com/INNO/WWI

INDEX